The Lazy Rooster

A Waverley Story Book for Children

Written by Amanda Stanford
Illustrated by Charlotte Moody and Kitty Van Oosten

The Reworkd Press
Charlotte, 2014

For Wee Evie

Just before dawn Rooster said, "I'm tired," and he did not crow.

So the Sun said, "I'm tired too," and it stayed dark.

So Cow slept and there was no milk.

And Chicken slept and there were no eggs.

And Farmer slept and no work was done.

"I'm hungry," said Rooster.

"COCK
DOO
DOO

-A-

-ODLE-

-OOOO!"

The Sun woke up; the Cow woke up.

COCK-
A - DOODLE -DOOOOo!

COCK-A- DOODLE DOOOO!

The Chicken woke up; the Farmer woke up.

And it was

morning.

About the author:

Dr. Amanda Stanford earned her PhD in English Creative Writing from the University of Edinburgh. She has taught writing and English classes for seven years in the US, Mexico, Japan, and Egypt. She also writes historical fiction under the pen name A M Montes de Oca.

About the illustrators:

Kitty Van Oosten is a self-taught illustrator and graphic novel artist, who obtained a degree in English Language, Literature and Culture from Leiden University before studying English Creative Writing at the University of Edinburgh. She currently teaches English at Tio University of Applied Sciences in the Netherlands. In her leisure time she writes and illustrates fiction, and hopes to publish her first novel in the near future.

Charlotte Moody studied art and art therapy at Capital University. Originally from Ohio, she now lives in Dallas, Texas, with her husband and wee pup, Popcorn.

www.ingramcontent.com/pod-product-compliance
Lightning Source LLC
Chambersburg PA
CBHW042100040426
42448CB00002B/78